Prescription for Peace

Sixty-second readings to help you build a better life

Steve Goodier

First Edition

Life Support System ♥ Publishing, Inc.
P.O. Box 237 Divide, CO 80814
www.LifeSupportSystem.com

Steve Goodier

Prescription for Peace

Sixty-second readings to help you build a better life

By Steve Goodier

Life Support System♡Publishing, Inc.
P.O. Box 237 Divide, CO 80814

Library of Congress Card Number: 00-191927

ISBN 1-929664-03-6 (Softcover)

Cover design: Brent Stewart & Darrel Voth

Contents

Dare to Believe

A veterinarian prescribed three huge pills to be given to a sick mule. "How do I get him to take the pills?" the farmer asked.

"It's quite simple," replied the vet. "Just insert the pill into a pipe. Put the pipe in the mule's mouth and blow on the other end. He will swallow the pill without realizing it."

The next day the farmer returned, looking sickly. "You look awful!" said the doctor. "What happened?" The farmer explained, "He blew first."

It occurs to me that some people will swallow anything! Maybe not literally, but it seems that some people are ready to believe in any new "get-rich" scheme; to follow any new fad; to swallow any fantastic story!

There is little merit in boasting an ability to "swallow" anything that comes along. Gullibility has never ranked high among the world's virtues. But, on the other hand, how much virtue is there in

1

believing nothing? Worthy lives are built around firmly held beliefs. It is rightly said that those who stand for nothing will likely fall for anything.

What do you stand for? In what do you passionately believe? Love? Generosity? Compassion? Forgiveness? Kindness? Joy? Peace? Loyalty? Faith? Integrity? Prayer? Work? Discipline? Beautiful beliefs build beautiful lives.

Do you want to know how to determine what you *really* believe? Observe how you habitually act. If you truly believe it, you will daily live it! If you believe in joy, you will usually be joyful. If you believe in generosity, you will be known as a generous person. Or if you believe in forgiveness, you will be one who readily gives a second chance. Your actions, not your words, tell the world what you truly believe.

Those beautiful beliefs will become the foundation for a beautiful life, for if you truly believe it, you will live it.

Go ahead...dare to believe!

We Can Get Bigger

I've never followed boxing closely, but I chuckle at the attitude of a high school boxing coach. Some of the new athletes were, let's say, better suited for other activities. One of his boys worked furiously for a couple of rounds, but never connected with anything that might be construed as a punch. Nevertheless, he asked, "What do you think, Coach? Have I done him any damage?"

"No," said a bewildered coach. "But keep on swinging. The draft might give him a cold."

Slim as it is, that might be his only chance to win! And we've all been there, haven't we? Slim to none are sometimes the best odds we can hold out for. And actually, sometimes it is better to keep on swinging – failure comes only *after* we have given up!

It took 32 years of failures for dedicated climbers to reach the top of Mt. Everest, a peak scaled so often now it hardly makes the newspaper!

At over 29,000 feet of altitude, snow never melts atop Mt. Everest. Sometimes winds at the summit reach 200 miles per hour.

George Leigh-Mallory is first recorded as attempting the climb in 1921. On his third try, in 1924, he disappeared into the mist, never to be seen alive again. The mountain had won. But friends of Mallory one day gazed upon a large picture of Mt. Everest and declared, "Mt. Everest, you defeated us once. You defeated us twice. You defeated us three times. But, Mt. Everest, we shall some day defeat you because you can't get any bigger – and we can!"

Eight more attempts were made on the mountain resulting in eight more failures. But finally, along came Edmund Hillary in 1953 who, along with his guide, Tenzing Norgay, reached the summit for the first time!

Failure comes only after one gives up. If slim to none are the odds of winning, they might be worth taking. For we can always get bigger – bigger in ability; bigger in experience; bigger in wisdom; bigger in faith.

I like the observation of Josh Billings, who says, "Consider the postage stamp: its usefulness consists in the ability to stick to one thing 'til it gets there!"

P.S.

Robert F. Kennedy reminded us that, "Only those who dare to fail greatly can ever achieve greatly."

Ending Up Where You Ought to Be

One man says it really happened. At the conclusion of his medical exam, the doctor asked him if he would please call in the next patient. So, as he opened the waiting room door, he called, "Mrs. Colchester, please."

He had walked some distance along the street outside when he heard Mrs. Colchester's voice behind him, "Where are we going?"

She was being called, but she misunderstood the intent. I only hope the poor lady didn't miss her appointment!

I can relate to her. I, too, have experienced "callings" in my life. I have felt led to pursue a certain vocation or direction. And I, too, have been confused at times about exactly where I am going when following my calling. Or where I may end up.

It's an old-fashioned word, "calling." It can mean a profession or line of work. Or even a strong inner urge or impulse. To follow a calling may be to do what you are meant to do or be where you are supposed to be.

It is a marvelous thing when one feels called. It may be to a role (a parent or a friend), or a job (even the most humble of jobs can be valid callings), or to volunteer service. It is a matter of doing something you believe you are meant to do. It is about following a voice that will lead you, if not always where you want to go, certainly where you are needed to go.

It is common not to know if, or to what, we are called. (And quite honestly, many don't care. Like one fashion consultant who recently said, "If you look good and dress well, you don't need a purpose in life." If it were only so!) But what a wonderful thing it is to find the spot where you are supposed to land.

Your life can be rich and satisfying when you follow your calling. Are you listening?

Who Cares?

In their book *The Big Book of Jewish Humor* (HarperCollins, 1981), William Novak and Moshe Waldoks tell of a woman from Brooklyn, New York, who, on her 80th birthday, decided to prepare her last will and testament. She went to her rabbi to make two final requests.

First, she insisted on cremation.

"What is your second request?" the rabbi asked.

"I want my ashes scattered over the Bloomingdale's store."

"Why Bloomingdale's?"

"Then I'll be sure that my daughters visit me twice a week," came the reply.

We all want to know that people care. We want to be sure that we are not alone in this world. For that reason, we are drawn to those who make us feel as if we matter.

I learned recently about a teacher named Robert Rasmussen, who has a unique way of showing concern to his students. He keeps a stuffed bear on his desk he calls the "Love Bear." He tells his high school students to come up and get the bear if they are feeling down or discouraged. Even the seniors!

At first, a few of the girls took the bear to their seats. The boys muttered among themselves, "Is he for real? I mean, go get a Teddy bear? Come on!" But after a while they came forward, too. Football players – six-and-a-half feet tall and weighing 220 pounds – now say to each other, "Gimme the bear!" and pass it among themselves.

Mr. Rasmussen has fine-tuned the art of showing concern to his students. When he spots a student who looks discouraged, he tosses the stuffed animal and says, "You look like you could use the bear." It is a way of saying "I care. I don't have time to spend with you right now – I have a lesson to teach – but I really do care. I'm with you."

Is it any surprise? Mr. Rasmussen was voted Teacher of the Year at his school four years straight.

Customers, colleagues, family and friends all need to know that we are concerned. They want to know who cares. And they will respond to us better when they feel that they matter.

Whatever else you tell people today, will you let them know who cares?

P.S.

"If a man is called to be a street-sweeper, he should sweep streets even as Michelangelo painted, or Beethoven composed music, or Shakespeare wrote poetry. He should sweep streets so well that all the hosts of heaven and earth will pause to say, 'Here lived a great street-sweeper who did his job well.'" ~ Dr. Martin Luther King, Jr.

Family Resemblance

"It's amazing to me," one woman said, "how so many people all around the world have the same problems, no matter where they are from. It's like we're one big family!"

I wonder, if we are family, is there a family resemblance? Is it simply that we are human, or are there some identifying characteristics that mark us as belonging to each other?

An unusual thing happened to me a few years ago. I spoke casually with a woman who served tables at a restaurant I frequented. We knew each other by first name only, but usually spoke to for a few minutes each time I dined there.

One day, she asked me, "Do you have a son about eight years old?"

"What has he done?" I thought. I nodded.

She pressed on, "Does he play soccer?"

When I said that he did, she asked if he played in a game the previous week at a particular field. Again, I answered, "Yes."

"I thought so," she smiled. "I saw him and thought he must be your son."

Since there were tens of thousands of young boys in the city, I was amazed! "I didn't know he looked that much like me!" I exclaimed.

"Oh, I didn't see his face," she said smiling as if she were keeping a secret.

"Then how did you know he was my son?" Now I was puzzled.

"I was just sitting in the car," she continued, "and I saw a little boy in a baseball cap walking across the field. *He walks like you!*"

When I told my son what she said he spent the next three weeks practicing a different walk! But it didn't work...it must be something that runs in the family.

In a greater sense, maybe the way we walk in this life is the identifying mark of the family. Some people walk in gentleness. Others walk in anger. Some walk in love, others in fear. Some walk in joy and some in peace, some in kindness and some in tolerance. Many walk in hope and in faith.

If we are family, then we are connected by common needs and hopes. These cannot be seen. But we will always be recognized by the way we walk!

When You're Root-Bound

Like potted plants, people can become "root- bound."

We have a beautiful "Christmas Cactus" which I gave to my wife as a gift 24 years ago. It has accompanied us through tough years and good times. It has lived with us in four different communities and has been present during the raising of our family. But it almost died.

As the small plant grew, we transferred it to a larger pot. It did well for about twenty years, but then began to die. It seemed that no amount of feeding, coddling or attention helped. We finally plucked a few leaves, re-rooted them and started over.

We could barely remove the now-dead plant from its pot for all the knotted and intertwined roots. The beautiful succulent was dying because it outgrew its environment. The plant changed, but the container it lived in stayed the same.

People, too, can die when they outgrow their environments. They need broader views, bigger challenges. Songwriter Bob Dylan put it this way: "If you are not busy being born, you are busy dying."

One man was offered employment at a salary higher than he had ever made in his life. After careful consideration, he declined the position.

"What's the matter?" his potential boss asked. "Isn't the salary big enough?"

"The salary is fine," the man said. "It's the job that's not big enough." He chose growth over decline, life over death.

Karen Kaiser Clark said, "Life is change... growth is optional...choose wisely."

Good advice − especially when we find ourselves becoming root-bound.

P.S.

"Women will never be equal to men," one *wit observed, "until they can walk down the street with a bald head and a beer gut and still think they are beautiful."*

Our Valuable Children

One proud father said to his little boy, "I've got news for you, my big boy. God has sent you a beautiful baby brother."

"Great!" yelped the little boy. "Where's Mom? I can't wait to tell her!"

His sister, however, wasn't nearly as excited about the arrival. After a few days her father asked, "Aren't you happy about having a new baby brother?"

"Not really," she admitted. "I wanted a little sister so we could play girl games when she got bigger. And we can't give him back. We've used him for five days."

However, she may yet grow to cherish her little brother. For children the world over should be cherished. They are, and always have been, our most valuable resource.

Peter De Vries has said, "The value of marriage is not that adults produce children, but that children produce adults." It's today's children who will be tomorrow's adults. We must treat them with the utmost care; we must responsibly educate and train our young people; we must, above all, show them the value of love for all people.

An unknown author put it succinctly: "A child is a person who is going to carry on what you have started. He or she is going to sit where you are sitting and attend to those things that you think are important. You may adopt all the policies you please, but how they will be carried out depends on our young people. They will assume control of your duties, states and nation. They are going to move in and take over your churches, schools, universities and corporations. All your books will be judged, praised or condemned by them. The fate of humanity is in their hands. So it might be well to pay young people attention."

Remember, the best thing to spend on your children is time. Today.

Skunks I've Run With

Ever run with a skunk?

A newspaper story once related that a mother of eight from Darlington, Maryland, had been visiting next door. When she returned home she went into the living room where she saw her five youngest children huddled in the center of the floor – on her new carpet – very much involved with something wiggly and squirmy. The perplexed mother looked closer. To her total dismay, she discovered that the children were gathered around a family of skunks.

In her horror she screamed, "Run, children, run!"

They did. Each child grabbed a skunk and ran.

I know I've sometimes made the same mistake. Instead of leaving a potentially smelly situation alone, I decided to "run" with it. Many of my problems have been the result of my own poor choices and bad judgment, though I may be tempted to blame someone else. A skunk I'll sometimes run with is "the easy way" when there may be a clear "better way" which seems just too difficult at the time. Another skunk is "instant gratification" – the I-want-it-now decision that often turns out to reek in the long run. Or I allow fear or guilt to influence my decisions, which almost always guarantees an outcome that stinks.

You see, many of my troubles are just the result of "stinking thinking." I really can't blame anyone or anything else. I get seduced by a furry, little skunk and run with it. But smelly decisions make for smelly problems. Better to run *from* those skunks than with them!

Like me, have you ever run with skunks? Or the more important question is...if you're running with one now, will you put it down? Our lives can smell pretty wonderful when we begin to make better decisions, and we'll have no one to blame for the improvement but ourselves!

P.S.

One newspaper ran an article on spending time with your child...under the unfortunate headline: **Include Your Children When Baking Cookies.**

A Great Word

I heard a funny story of an ancient monastery charged with copying old books and scrolls for the faith.

One day, Father Florian, who headed the work of the scriptorium, was asked by a new monk: "Does not the copying by hand of other copies allow for chances of error? How do we know we are not copying the mistakes of someone else? Are they ever checked against the originals?"

"A very good point," Father Florian agreed. "I will take one of the latest books down to the vault and compare it to the original."

After a day had passed and the priest had not returned, the monks began to worry. When they went to the vault, they found him weeping over an ancient manuscript.

"What is the problem, Father?" asked one of the monks.

"A mistake," he sobbed. "The word was supposed to be *'celebrate!'*"

We can be assured that "celibate" was never confused with "celebrate," but do we tend to leave celebration out of spirituality? For some people, it is all about following the rules and practices. For others, it is a celebration of love.

Would you say your life is more like a guest at a party, or like the one who cleans up after someone else's party? Would the joy of a friend's wedding or the obligation of yet another committee meeting more closely describe your approach to living?

Not that we can be, or ought to be, happy all the time. There is much growth in pain. But "celebrate" is one of those great words that leads to great living. If you think you could use more celebration, today is a *great* day to begin!

Under Construction

I have been on a self-improvement program most of my life. Though I realize I am continually under construction and will never be fully completed in a lifetime, I relate to the poet who set these words to paper:

"Your task is to build a better world,"
said God, and I questioned, "How?
This world is such a vast place and, oh,
so complicated now. And I am so small
and useless, there is nothing I can do."
But God in all great wisdom said,
"You just build a better you."

That was the strategy of the Greek orator Demosthenes some two thousand years ago. Speaker and author, Nido Qubein, in the book *Communicate Like a Pro* (Prentice-Hall, Inc., 1983), tells that Demosthenes lived in the "golden

23

age of orators," when public disputes were settled by oration. As a young man, he was given the chance to speak to the assembly on some vital issue. But his weak voice trembled, his thoughts were muddled and he grew less confident as the speech progressed. He was finally forced to step down to the sound of boos and hisses. Humiliated, he withdrew from public life.

But the young man was not easily defeated. More than anything, Demosthenes wanted to be a great orator. So he launched his own self-improvement program. To improve his diction, he practiced for hours at a time with stones in his mouth. To strengthen his weak voice, he shouted over the heavy winds blowing in from the Aegean Sea. To clarify his presentation, he studied the techniques of the masters. And to overcome his fears, he practiced with a sharp sword hanging over his head!

An opportunity came again several years later, and this time he was ready. He stepped in front of the assembly to warn the national leaders of the great threat posed by Philip II of Macedonia. He offered concise ideas as to how they should fight this dangerous intruder. So powerful was his speech and so clear were his thoughts that, when he had finished, the entire audience rose as one person shouted, "Let us go and fight Philip!"

You may have no desire to become a great public speaker. But, if you're like me, there will always be plenty of room for improvement in areas to which you are well-suited. And if you patiently develop and refine your skills, if you hang out the "Under Construction" sign and persistently build a better you, you will be ready when the right time comes. And you will be unstoppable.

P.S.

Money takes the sting out of being poor....

Grow Antennae

A story, which may be relegated to the files of "urban legends," tells about a Philadelphia legal firm that sent flowers to an associate in Baltimore upon the opening of its new offices. Through some mix-up, the ribbon that bedecked the floral piece read, "Deepest Sympathy."

When the florist was duly informed of her mistake, she let out a cry of alarm. "Good grief! Then the flowers that went to the funeral said, "Congratulations On Your New Location!"

It is difficult enough to offer comfort without mixing up the sentiment! So difficult, in fact, that many people simply don't know what to say to someone who has just unburdened grief or emotional pain. Not unlike the new clergyman who, when a distressed young woman confided that she was pregnant, blurted out, "Are you sure it's yours?"

27

Too often, we want to help, but find that our attempts to offer comfort, solace or hope fall short of the mark. But there *is* something we can say that can be helpful.

One man, whose grandson died accidentally, found genuine comfort when he shared his pain with friends shortly after the tragedy. Of all the well-meaning words of support, two statements helped to sustain and comfort him through the grief more than the rest. They were: "Thank you for sharing your pain," and "I grieve with you." After hearing those words, he no longer felt alone in his suffering. He felt as if his friends embraced his grief. He felt better.

We can't fix it. We shouldn't try to offer advice. And we may never know how someone feels who is hurting in a way we have never experienced. But we *can* give some comfort.

I think James Angell, former president of the University of Michigan, got it right when he was asked the secret of his success. "The secret of success?" he replied. "Grow antennae, not horns."

Let the Past Be Past

Is it difficult for you to forgive? To let the past be past? It is for me. Nearly impossible sometimes. I'm a little like the elderly Virginian woman who lived to see her beloved Richmond occupied by Union troops after the American Civil War. The matron was walking down a Richmond street when she tripped over a step and fell. A Union soldier courteously helped her up.

"How very kind of you, young man," she said acidly. "If there is a cool spot in hell, I hope you get it."

Maybe it was still a bit early for her to let go of those deep-seated resentments. But angry and bitter lives are never happy lives.

A beautiful legend tells of an African tribe that ritualizes forgiveness. When a tribe member acts irresponsibly or unjustly, he/she is taken to the center of the village. All work ceases and every man, woman and child in the village gathers in a large circle around the accused. Then the tribe bombards the rejected person with affirmations! One at a time, friends and family enumerate all the good the individual has done. Every incident, every experience that can be recalled with some detail and accuracy is recounted. All their positive attributes, strengths and kindnesses are recited carefully and at length. Finally, the tribal circle is broken, a joyous celebration takes place, and the outcast is welcomed back into the tribe.

What a beautiful ritual of restoration! They replace hurt with happiness; pain with peace. Once again they are family. The rejected one is restored and the village is made whole.

Paul Boese has said, "Forgiveness does not change the past, but it does enlarge the future." As brothers and sisters in our global village, is letting go of those resentments really an option?

P.S.

Kindness is catching. Pass it on.

Way to Results

Melodie Hartline relates in *Reader's Digest* (September 1996) that in her job as an employee of a jewelry store, she often arranged for engaged couples to have their wedding bands engraved with something special. She once asked a bride-to-be what she would like inscribed inside her fiancé's ring.

"We aren't very romantic," she replied. Then she related that they were marrying on her fiancé's birthday so he wouldn't forget the date!

Melodie persisted, "Isn't there something you'll want him to remember as he looks inside his ring?"

"There sure is," she said. And that's how "*Put it back on!*" came to be inscribed inside her husband's ring.

Perhaps she was trying to "help along" her husband's commitment to the relationship....

Catherine, from Scotland, may have wanted to help along her lover's commitment for several decades. And finally, her 68-year-old boyfriend, George, proposed after 44 years of courtship. Why the wait? "He is a bit shy, you know," Catherine said.

At the heart of any meaningful relationship is commitment. Further, commitment is vital to the success of *any* endeavor. Happy people are committed people. They commit to other people, they commit to themselves, they commit to God, and they commit to their dreams. They know that nothing is possible without firm resolve.

Author Ken Blanchard has said, "There's a difference between interest and commitment. When you're interested in doing something, you do it only when it's convenient. When you're committed to something, you accept no excuses – only results."

What about you? Are you ready for results?

The Way You Say It!

Walking into a noisy classroom, the teacher slapped her hand on the desk and ordered sharply, "I *demand* pandemonium!" The class quieted down immediately. "It isn't what you demand," she later explained, "but the way you demand it."

It isn't always what you say, but the way you say it. Try saying, "I love you," with a scowl!

An international tourist came upon a group of people listening to an orator in the central square of a small European town. The speaker shouted from a makeshift podium. At one point, his arms waved about wildly, his stern face turned red and the veins in his neck were bulging.

Since he could not speak the language, the now curious tourist asked a man next to him what the speaker was ranting about. The man pointed to a church spire in the distance and said, "See that church steeple? The fellow who is speaking in the square is the pastor of that church. Right now he is preaching about the love of God!"

It isn't always what you say, but the way you say it. One marriage counselor sometimes asks couples who have difficulty communicating to forget words and take 20 minutes and simply look into each other's face and be silent together. They may see what they have missed: hurting eyes, longing hearts, unfulfilled dreams, unmet needs, or a yearning to love and be loved. They learn that deep communication is more than words.

Who needs to hear what is in your heart? *How* you share it will be as important as the words you use.

P.S.

Having children will turn you into your parents.

Mad Dash

This is the age
Of the half-read page.
And the quick hash
And the mad dash.
The bright night
With the nerves tight.
The plane hop
With the brief stop.
The lamp tan
In a short span.
The Big Shot
In a good spot.
And the brain strain
The heart pain.
And the cat naps
Till the spring snaps —
And the fun's done!

Sound familiar? But wait – this poem was actually published in The Saturday Evening Post in 1949, under the title, "Time of the Mad Atom." Seems that people were as rushed then as they are now!

Personally, I like the father who decided to slow down and spend some afternoon time walking with his son. The inquisitive boy used the opportunity to satisfy his curiosity on a few subjects he'd been thinking about.

"How does electricity go through those telephone wires, Dad?" he asked.

His father replied, "I don't know. I never knew much about electricity, Son."

A few blocks further the boy asked, "What causes lightning and thunder?"

"To tell you the truth," came the reply, "I never understood that myself."

A bit later he asked, "Why do some leaves turn red and others turn yellow in the Fall?"

"I'm not really sure, Son," his father answered.

Finally, as they were nearing home, the boy said, "Dad, I hope you don't mind my asking you so many questions."

"Of course not!" exclaimed his father. "How else are you going to learn?"

Maybe the old man wasn't a walking encyclopedia, but you have to hand it to him, he invested some time listening and talking to his son. Which may be far more valuable than rattling off accurate answers to questions! The message he gave his boy was: "You are important to me and I want to spend time with you." It's a matter of finding time.

Whether these are the worst of times or the best of times, these are the only times we've got. Today, will you find time for that which is valuable?

You Are One of Us

Salt Lake City, Utah, is a worldwide center for genealogical research. Even the big department stores sell genealogy supplies.

One newcomer to Salt Lake City, and a non-researcher, got a job as a clerk at one of those big department stores. She received her introduction to genealogy one day when a customer came into the store and asked, "Where do I find the family group sheets?"

The new clerk, with a shocked look on her face, answered, "Family group sheets? All we carry are the king, queen, double and twin-size sheets."

Maybe family sized bedding is taking closeness a bit far! But having family or close friends is one of the essential needs of all people. We long for emotional support and intimacy.

Most of us are familiar with studies that have shown that people suffering from cancer or vascular problems have a higher survival rate when they enjoy a strong support system of family and friends. People need people.

Moreover, a supportive wider community can also be important. Not long ago, scores of people gathered on a California beach, lighting candles and lifting voices in song. Mostly strangers to one another, they came there to grieve the loss of 88 persons who died when a jetliner crashed into the ocean off their coast. They were not even family and friends of the victims – simply concerned residents who cared.

"Your joy, your pain, your loss, your gain – are ours...for you are one of us." That is the powerful message of family. At its best, even an Internet family can help fill our need for closeness. Your joy, your pain, your loss, your gain – can be shared. You belong. And together, we'll celebrate it! Or, we will get through it.

P.S.

Friends are God's way of taking care of us.

Look Upon Them As Wounded

After vaccinating a young boy with an injection in the arm, a doctor wanted to stick on a bandage. "Please put it on the other arm," the boy pleaded.

"Why do that?" the doctor asked. "This will let everyone know you have been vaccinated and they won't hit your sore arm."

"Please put it on my other arm! Please!" the boy begged. "You don't know the kids at my school."

He couldn't show his weakness. He was afraid to let others know of his vulnerability for fear of being hurt more than he was already.

Adults, too, are pretty good at hiding pain. Not usually physical pain, but the pain of loss or rejection or fear. They like to appear as if they are in control; they can handle whatever life throws them; they're on top of it. And, too often, they end up going it alone. No one understands. No one is there to help.

Susan Muto, in her book *Blessings That Make Us Be* (Crossroad, 1982), tells a story of a great ruler who needed a second-in-command to help manage his kingdom. When he finally selected the right person, he took him outside onto a balcony of the palace where they could gaze over all the lands under his jurisdiction. His assistant asked the king, "Master, what must I remember most of all if I am to carry out your wishes?"

"My son," the king replied, "there is only one directive to follow – and that is to look upon the people as wounded."

The wise king knew that everyone is in pain in some way. Wounds may not show, but they are there.

Discover where people hurt and you'll finally understand them. Learn where the invisible bandages are and you'll know how to help, heal or reach them. Look upon them as wounded – and you'll know what to do.

Volunteer Victims

It's a great temptation to volunteer as a victim. Do you know that we sign up for that job?

A man who dined regularly in his favorite restaurant complained about the bread. It wasn't fair, he emphasized, that other restaurants served lots of bread. But here he gets only one piece.

So the next time he came in, they served him four pieces. He still complained it wasn't enough.

On his next visit his server brought him a dozen pieces of bread. The man still complained.

For his next visit they put a large basket of bread on the table. But still he complained. "The other restaurants give all the bread you can eat."

They decided to be ready for him the next day. They had an enormous loaf of bread prepared. It was six feet long and two feet wide. Four people carried the loaf to his table. They plopped it down in front of him. It took up half the table and hung over both sides. The chef stood back, pleased with himself, to see how the customer would react.

He looked over the loaf and commented, "So, we're back to one piece again, are we?"

Like this man, we volunteer to be victims, but in more subtle ways. We believe life is unfair, people are untrustworthy and we are getting a bad shake. We think everyone should know just how terrible things are and we feel obliged to tell them.

One man says of a friend that he hates to ask her how she is feeling because he knows ahead of time what she will say. "You get an organ recital from her," he says. She dwells on her health problems to the exclusion of everything good in her life.

The problem is, life sometimes *is* unfair and we can be victimized. But the greater truth is, people can decide whether they are victims or are victors. They can feel helpless and miserable, or they can try to feel strong. Happy people have learned that they cannot always control their circumstances, but they can often control how they will respond.

Lewis Dunning said, "What life means to us is determined not so much by what life brings to us as by the attitude we bring to life; not so much by what happens to us as by our reaction to what happens."

You were born to be a victor! You were meant to be happy! Will you claim your birthright today?

P.S.

"It isn't what you have, or who you are, or where you are, or what you are doing that makes you happy or unhappy. It's what you think about!" ~ *Dale Carnegie (1888-1955)*

Web of Love

Listen to how a simple ball of yarn became a web of love for one classroom of high school students.

Their teacher seated the students in a circle on the carpeted floor. One member of the group was instructed to toss a ball of yarn to someone across the circle, holding tightly to one end. The recipient took hold of the string and listened as the one who tossed it shared something that she especially liked about him. Keeping hold of the string, he then tossed the ball across the circle to someone else and affirmed something positive about her. The ball of yarn was tossed across and around the circle until everyone had both heard and shared encouragement...and thus the yarn became a woven web of love and good feelings....

Before they went their separate ways, the teacher took scissors and snipped through the web. Each person took a piece of yarn away as a remembrance of the special words they heard. Surprisingly, many of them wore cherished pieces of yarn around their wrists for days and weeks afterward.

Every year now, students ask their teacher to end the term with the *Web of Love*. It has become an annual tradition in their high school! Which goes to show how much encouragement means to most people.

Why wait? We can find opportunities to affirm others throughout the day. Few people grow weary of hearing sincere appreciation and praise. And each time you give it you help to create an invisible web of love that can last a lifetime.

Your Own Best Friend

Most people report that they do not usually feel confident. But exciting things can happen when we actually believe in ourselves. Here is a man who believed in his own ability even as a boy, and that confidence helped shape his adult life.

At the turn of the last century, a young boy quit school to help with the family expenses. When he was fifteen, he became interested in automobiles and worked in a garage. He subscribed to a correspondence home study course on automobiles and, after a long day in the garage, studied at the kitchen table by lamplight.

When he felt ready, he walked into the Frayer-Miller Automobile Company of Columbus, Ohio. When Mr. Frayer noticed him, he asked, "Well, what do you want?"

"I just thought I'd tell you I'm coming to work here tomorrow morning," the boy replied.

"Oh! Who hired you?"

"Nobody yet, but I'll be on the job in the morning. If I'm not worth anything, you can fire me." (Try *that* in today's market!)

Early the next morning the young man returned to the plant. Noticing the floor was thick with metal shavings and accumulated dirt and grease, the boy got a broom and shovel and set to work cleaning the place.

Because of his self-confidence and work ethic, Eddie Rickenbacker's future was predictable. He went on to excel in many fields, including automobile racing, piloting World War 1 planes and founding what was to become one of America's largest airline companies – Eastern Airlines.

There is no magic bullet to instantly become a self-confident person. But it begins with one of the most important relationships in your life – your relationship with yourself. People who become more confident habitually encourage themselves. They become their own best friend.

Rob Bremer asks the question, "If you had a friend who talked to you like you sometimes talk to yourself, would you continue to hang around with that person?" If the answer is "Yes!" you are on the track to becoming more self-assured.

Without confidence, you are not likely to move far in the direction of your dreams. But become your own best friend and almost anything will be possible.

P.S.

Saying enough without saying too much can be tricky. A prayer I learned years ago puts it well: "Lord, fill my mouth with worthwhile stuff. And nudge me when I have said enough."

Love and Romance!

An old story reminds us of the humor of romance. A man was going to the county fair one day with a pig under one arm and a chicken under the other arm and a basket on his head. He came to a crossroads and didn't know which way to turn. While he stood there deciding, a young woman approached him, heading the same direction.

"Please, ma'am, I'm on the way to the county fair. Can you tell me which way to go?"

"Yes," she replied. "I'm on my way there, too. We'll go right down this way about a mile, turn left about a mile and a half, left again about a mile and we're right there."

He said, "Wait a minute...down here, turn left and left again? Couldn't we save a lot of time by walking through these woods?"

She replied, "Yes, we could. But I couldn't walk through those woods with you. Why...you might try to kiss me!"

"Listen," he said, "how could I possibly kiss anybody with a pig under one arm, a chicken under the other arm, and a basket on my head?"

"Well, you could put that chicken on the ground, turn the basket upside down over the chicken, and I could hold that little bitty ole pig."

Where there is love, there's a way! Although one would be hard-pressed to define a romantic attraction as "love." They are really not at all the same things. And as nice as it is to keep romance in our lives, in the end, isn't it love which we are really after?

Writer Marjorie Holmes points out the difference between love and romance: "Romance is seeking perfection; love is forgiving faults. Romance is flying; love is a safe landing. Romance is the anguish of waiting for the phone to ring to bring you a voice that will utter endearments; love is the anguish of waiting for a call that will assure you someone else is happy and safe. Romance is eager, striving always to appear attractive for each other; love is two people who find beauty in each other no matter how they look."

Authentic love will find many expressions – the love of spouses; the love of friends; the love of families. It doesn't require one to be "in love" and will likely grow over the years.

Romance is wonderful, but love is essential. Are you filling your life with love?

The Applause that Refreshes

"Do you think my hair is soft and shiny?" Jessica asked Josh one moonlit evening.

Josh answered, "Yep."

"And are my eyes bright and beautiful?" she continued.

"Yep," he replied.

After a few minutes Jessica forged ahead, "Josh, do you think my skin is smooth and clear?"

"Yep."

At this, Jessica smiled brightly and declared, "Oh, Josh, you say the sweetest things!"

No relationship can be built on flattery, but sincere compliments smooth over many rough edges. A thoughtful compliment is a way of saying, "I care enough to notice." Even relationships that are *not* romantic in nature will benefit from well-placed compliments.

Granted, some people feel suspicious, embarrassed, or defensive when complimented. They sometimes suspect that fine words might be part of a manipulative design. And quite often, people respond to compliments with mixed emotions rather than plain gratitude, primarily because they find the sincerity behind them suspect.

But most often, *sincere* encouragement can bolster self-confidence and cement friendships. In love relationships, thoughtful compliments can help keep the fires of romance burning vigorously.

One marriage counselor says, "Compliment your spouse at least once every day." He cautions against flattery by adding, "It should be sincere. Then point out something *new* you appreciate about him or her every week. Make sure it is something you have never mentioned before. You'll be surprised at what it does for your marriage."

Compliments cost nothing and can accomplish so much. They are the applause that refreshes.

P.S.

A pat on the back is only a few vertebrae from a kick in the pants, but it's miles ahead in results.

The Most Important Trip You May Ever Take

It is accurately said that it is easy to be an angel when nobody ruffles your feathers. But it seems that feather rufflers will always be around.

We're told that 19th Century German statesman Prince Otto von Bismarck once became so incensed at the criticism of a professor (he must have ruffled the prince's feathers), that he challenged him to a duel. Protocol had it that the one challenged was to have the choice of weapons.

The professor made his choice...sausages! He sent word to Bismarck, along with a pair of sausages, that one sausage was safe to eat. The other had been poisoned with trichinae, which would cause a slow and lingering death, or at least long invalidism. He informed the prince that he should choose which sausage to eat and said he would eat the other one.

Bismarck reasoned that a man might die with some sort of honor on a dueling field, but never by food poisoning. He sent the message back, "His highness has destroyed the sausages and asks that you be his guest at dinner this evening. After due consideration he feels he may have been slightly in error. He believes an agreement can be reached."

One of the most important trips a person ever takes is "to meet someone halfway." Bismarck met his adversary halfway and chose to bring something useful from his conflict.

When others ruffle our feathers, we always have a choice. We can meet them on the dueling field, where one will clearly win and the other will lose, or we can meet them halfway. Even armed only with words, we can seek to hurt or we can seek a solution.

The choice we make will make all the difference.

The Black Belt

A parable tells about a martial artist who kneels before a master sensei in a ceremony to receive the hard-earned Black Belt. After years of relentless training, the student has finally reached a pinnacle of achievement in the discipline.

"Before granting the belt, you must pass one more test," the sensei solemnly tells the young man.

"I'm ready," responds the student, expecting perhaps one more round of sparring.

"You must answer the essential question: What is the true meaning of the Black Belt?"

"Why, the end of my journey," says the student. "A well-deserved reward for my hard work."

The master waits for more. Clearly, he is not satisfied. The sensei finally speaks: "You are not ready for the Black Belt. Return in one year."

As the student kneels before his master a year later, he is again asked the question, "What is the true meaning of the Black Belt?"

"It is a symbol of distinction and the highest achievement in our art," the young man responds.

Again the master waits for more. Still unsatisfied, he says once more: "You are not ready for the Black Belt. Return in one year."

A year later the student kneels before his sensei and hears the question, "What is the true meaning of the Black Belt?"

This time he answers, "The Black Belt represents not the end, but the beginning, the start of a never-ending journey of discipline, work and the pursuit of an ever higher standard."

"Yes," says the master. "You are now ready to receive the Black Belt and begin your work."

You may not be hoping for a Black Belt, but you might be at a crucial point. Maybe you're facing a life change, perhaps even a painful one. Or maybe you are awaiting something you have worked hard to attain – graduation, a new job, a promotion, or even retirement.

All wise people see that changes can be new beginnings. Change need not be feared. And neither should we be looking for a permanent resting place, for a full and happy life is never stagnant.

Does the change you face represent, not just an ending, but a new beginning in your life's journey? If so, you may be ready to move forward.

P.S.

Speaking of change, Ashleigh Brilliant says, "My opinions may have changed, but not the fact that I am right."

Advice that Rings True

An efficiency expert once concluded his lecture with the comment, "Please don't try these techniques at home."

"Why not?" he was asked.

"I used to watch my wife prepare breakfast and wondered why she made so many trips to the table carrying only one item at a time," he replied. "One day I asked her, 'Wouldn't it be quicker and more efficient if you organized yourself to carry several things to the table at once?'"

"Did it work?" he was asked.

"Oh, yes, it worked," the expert replied. "It used to take my wife twenty minutes to prepare breakfast. Now I do it in seven."

Not all advice is readily received. And sometimes it is not heard the way it was intended. But neither should all advice be followed; rather, wisdom learns to separate kernels of truth from weeds.

Some advice worthy of consideration, though, comes from one of the richest people in the United States, offered to 380 high school students in Omaha, Nebraska. Here are five suggestions multi-billionaire Warren Buffett gave his audience:

1. Avoid credit cards. If you are going to make progress, you will not do it by borrowing at 18 to 20 percent interest.

2. Develop integrity, which guides intelligence and energy. Buffett said he looks for these three qualities in hiring people. "If they don't have the first one, integrity, the other two will kill you."

3. Establish good habits, picking people to admire and following their example, while learning to weed out attributes that are not admirable. "If you do that," he admonished, "two or three years from now you'll find out the person you admire most will be yourself."

4. Learn about companies before investing in them; do not rely on someone else's advice.

5. Choose professions for love of the work, not money.

My "Internet" friend, Alan Hillman, who sent this list, adds an excellent comment: "I believe the same advice is true for all of us, even someone like me who is about to enter my sixth decade of life. Seven years ago I decided to do what I loved most — loving people. Since that time my cup has slowly been filled and is now flowing over the brim with love. Simultaneously, while seeking humility and significance, I lost pride and prominence. In the meantime, I became debt-free and have a high six-figure net worth.

"During those seven years I have had several mottoes. Probably the most significant one is: If you are not loving life, you are not living love."

Some advice just rings true. The wise will follow.

Follow Your Stars

"Learn to say no," said Charles Spurgeon. "It will be of more use to you than to be able to read Latin."

One educator used to say that no society can last long unless it has a quorum of "unpurchasable people." These are people of principle who cannot be bought; people who have learned to say no. I believe that these so-called unpurchasable people are the truly contented and fulfilled souls around us.

In Whitney Seymour's book *Making A Difference* (New York: William Morrow and Co., Inc., 1984), Arthur McArthur, General Douglas McArthur's father, told his son of such an unpurchasable man. This man was a Union general in charge of the occupied territory surrounding New Orleans toward the end of the American Civil War. He was pressed by local plantation owners to permit them to haul their cotton to the wharves in order for it to be sold for shipment to England. The general controlled all the wagons and horses, and his orders from high command in Washington were clear. He was not to let the cotton crop get to market.

Then one day, when Colonel Arthur MacArthur was visiting the general, two Southern ladies were ushered into the general's office, a "grande dame" and a beautiful young companion. The older lady came right to the point. She said that the landowners needed the temporary use of transport facilities to move their cotton. The North did not wish to force England into the war, she argued, and was allowing some merchant ships to slip through the blockade. Therefore, the Union would not be opposed to the sale of cotton for English textile mills. To show her gratitude she handed over $250,000 in gold certificates. "And if you need other inducements, this young lady will supply them," she added. They departed, leaving behind a distressed general holding the beautiful young woman's address.

The general immediately ordered MacArthur to dispatch this message to Washington: "TO THE PRESIDENT OF THE UNITED STATES: I have just been offered two hundred and fifty thousand dollars and the most beautiful woman I have ever seen to betray my trust. I am depositing the money with the Treasury of the United States, and request immediate relief from this command. They are getting close to my price."

67

Many others may have fallen for the seductive offer. And though his decision was no doubt difficult to make, how much harder might his life have eventually become had he chosen wrong? Saying yes to contentment and peace often begins with saying no. For ultimately happy lives are guided by unwavering principles, such as honesty, trust and love. Those who keep sight of their principles and use them as a guide in all their decision-making will eventually arrive at a place of lasting peace.

"Ideals are like stars; you will not succeed in touching them with your hands," says Carl Schurz. "But like the (seafarers) on the desert of waters, you choose them as your guides, and following them you will reach your destiny."

P.S.

Don't worry about temptation -- as you grow older, it starts avoiding you. ~ Old Farmer's Almanac

The Meaning of Success

One man began a speech to his fellow college alumni with the statement, "Some of you are successes, and some of you are failures -- only God knows which are which!" There are many kinds of successes, many kinds of winners; and which is which may not at first be apparent.

Esther Kim is a true champion with a heart-warming story. She competed against her childhood friend, Kay Poe, in the U.S. Olympic Trials for her sport -- Taekwondo. Esther lost the match, but she went on to win all her other fights, which still qualified her for the finals.

Her friend, Kay, also won her successive matches. But in her last fight before the finals, disaster struck. Kay dislocated her knee and went down in great pain. Her knee was reset as she lay in agony on the mat. All the while, her friend Esther encouraged her from the sidelines to finish the fight.

Courageously, Kay finally stood up and, on one good leg, concluded the match for a win.

The only contestants now remaining were Kay Poe, with an injured leg, and her friend, Esther Kim. One woman would be chosen from these trials for the Olympic team. "I looked at her with one good leg against me with two good legs," Esther Kim recalled, "and I said, 'It's not fair!'"

On the spot, Esther made a hard decision. She forfeited the match to her friend Kay, whose leg was sure to be fully healed for the 2000 Olympic Games. For her part, Kay bought Esther a ticket to Sydney, Australia, so she might watch and cheer from the stands.

"This was our dream, going to the Olympics," Esther said. *"It's so hard!"* I have cried about it." But Esther discovered something important. "I gave her my dream," she said, "but for the first time ever, I feel like a champ." Esther Kim won a victory far greater than one fought on the mats. She won a victory of the spirit, which qualifies her as a true champion.

As Kay Poe's father remarked, "The champions aren't always the ones who have all the medals." No, sometimes they are cheering from the sidelines. For success and winning is often about victories won in the hidden recesses of the heart. And any of us who will fight and win such a victory will know the meaning of the word "success."

When Words Sting

A funny story tells of a hostess making final arrangements for an elaborate reception. "Nora," she said to her veteran servant, "for the first half-hour I want you to stand at the drawing room door and call the guests' names as they arrive."

Nora's face lit up. "Thank you, ma'am," she replied. "I've been wanting to do that to some of your friends for the last twenty years."

Maybe we can relate, but either manners or fear of losing a job kept us from saying what we felt at the time. Often better to do as Napoleon Hill suggests: "If you must slander someone, don't speak it – but write it – write it in the sand, near the water's edge!"

Criticism is not to be confused with evaluation. We would do well to have our performance evaluated from time to time. None of us is beyond improvement. But hurtful and self-serving criticism, often spoken out of anger or vindictiveness, creates irreparable damage in a relationship. From time to time, we each feel its sting.

Phillips Brooks, over a century ago, used to pray for the grace to both rise above criticisms as well as to resist firing them back. "Oh, God," he prayed, "give the strength to live another day. Keep me from losing faith in people. Keep me sweet and sound, in spite of occasional ingratitude and meanness. Above all, keep me from giving little stings, and minding them."

A good antidote when words sting.

Not-So-Grim Reaper

Cyrus McCormick, who invented the reaper and founded the company that became International Harvester, was a generous contributor to Chicago's Presbyterian Theological School. Because of that fact, the school later changed its name to McCormick Theological Seminary. Faculty and students have quipped that death is never referred to as "The Grim Reaper" at McCormick, but always as "The International Harvester."

"Grim" is not a word which describes the experience of many people who find themselves nearing life's end. Like Dr. Abraham Maslow commented after a heart attack which made him realize that his own death was not far away: "Death, and its ever-present possibility makes love, passionate love, more possible. I wonder if we could love passionately, if ecstasy would be possible at all, if we knew we'd never die."

Likewise, psychiatrist Irvin Yalom, who worked with terminally ill cancer patients, reported that "grimness" was far from their attitudes about passing on. In Dr. Chris Thurman's book, *The Truths We Must Believe* (Thomas Nelson Publishers, 1991), Yalom tells us that once his patients accepted the fact that their lives were rapidly drawing to an end, positive and exciting changes occurred:

❖ They felt a sense of freedom to do what they wanted to do.
❖ They lived in, and enjoyed, the present.
❖ They learned to vividly appreciate the world around them.
❖ They joyously anticipated holidays.
❖ They communicated deeper with loved ones.
❖ They feared less and risked more.

Because these people knew they were dying, they figured out how to live! Nothing grim here. They came alive in ways never before possible.

Oh, maybe you don't want to volunteer to leave this life today, but we'll each set off on that journey soon enough. And it promises to be an exciting adventure. But in the meantime, what if you set out to live every moment as if your short days here were truly numbered? When "The International Harvester" someday reaps your life, may it have been joyful, fearless and well-lived.

75

P.S.

Someone said, "Never knock on Death's door -- ring the doorbell and run. (He hates that)."

Decision Is Destiny

"Mommy, what happens when a car gets too old and banged up to run?" a little girl asked.

"Well," her mother said, "someone sells it to your father."

I think I have bought a couple of cars like that! Like most people, my life is punctuated by decisions that did not turn out the way I'd hoped. But we cannot always be expected to make the *best* decisions. Sometimes we simply don't have enough information. And other times, there just isn't a good decision anywhere to be found! All we can really do is make decisions the best way we know how and act on them. Things change only when decisions change.

Before his rise to political fame, Maryland Congressman Kweisi Mfume walked a path of self-destruction. He dropped out of high school. A few years later, he robbed a pedestrian in order to join a street gang. Mfume spent the following years drinking and troublemaking with the gang.

A turning point came one summer night when he abruptly decided he could no longer continue on his present course. He decided to earn his high school equivalency certificate and later graduated magna cum laude from Morgan State University in Baltimore. He then went on to earn a graduate degree at Johns Hopkins University.

When Mfume ran for Congress in 1986, his opponents tried to use his old mistakes against him. But his achievements since he left a troubled past behind captivated an electorate who voted him into office by an overwhelming 87 percent. He was on a collision course with total failure until he made a decision.

What changes your life is not learning more, though education is important. What changes your life is making decisions – the best decisions you can make – and acting on them. It's been accurately said: "Your decisions determine your direction, and your direction determines your destiny." Or put another way, "The decisions you make... make you."

No Room for Fences

You may know that Jackie Robinson was one of the first African Americans to play major league baseball. In his first season with the Brooklyn Dodgers, Robinson faced hostility nearly everywhere he traveled because of his race. Pitchers threw fastballs at his head. Runners spiked him on the bases. Brutal epithets were written on cards and shouted by players in the opposing dugouts. Even the home crowds in Brooklyn saw him as an object of reproach.

During one game in Boston, the taunts and racial slurs seemed to reach a peak. To make matters worse, Robinson committed an error and stood at second base humiliated while fans hurled insults at him. Another Dodger, a Southern white man by the name of "Pee Wee" Reese, called timeout. He walked over to Robinson and, with the crowds looking on, put his arm around his friend's shoulder. The fans grew quiet. Robinson later said that arm around his shoulder saved his career. Jackie Robinson eventually went on to become one of baseball's all-time greats.

An arm around his shoulder made the difference. It said to the crowd and anyone who cared to notice, "We are one."

Though we have made headway, race still divides us. As does religion and politics and ideologies. And, though we are learning better how to "put our arms" around people who are different, our global community is not yet unified.

It's been said, "There is just enough room in the world for all the people in it, but there is no room for the fences which separate them."

P.S.

Sometimes it is difficult to get along with those we are closest to. As one child said, "My brother and sister were in one of those Christmas plays at church. I couldn't help but think, 'Man, this play must be fiction, because my sister is an angel and my brother is a wise man.'"

Detours Are Temporary

In Death Valley, California, there is a place known as Dante's View. From there you can look down to the lowest spot in the United States, a depression in the earth 200 feet below sea level called Bad Water. But you can also look up to the highest peak in the contiguous United States, Mt. Whitney, which rises to a height of 14,500 feet.

Our lives also bring us to such places — where we can either journey into the depths of despair and depression or rise to incredible heights — depending on the direction we head. Yet, the mountaintop may not be where we want to reside, either. In a letter to a suicidal person, Al Hillman shared some exquisite wisdom:

"Sheila," he wrote, "I know all too well the battle you are engaged in. You see, I spent many years in the deep, dark valleys of mental illness. Most (people) want to be on the mountaintop. I don't. I have climbed mountains up to 17,000 feet.

Not a pleasant place to be. Bitterly cold, roaring winds, nothing grows there. Just snow, ice and rocks. Very uncomfortable. Even the view is dismal, for all one can see is clouds.

"I have also been in the deep, dark valleys where the walls are so steep that nothing grows; there is complete darkness and one is all alone. A terrifying place to be.

"I enjoy being in the valley (with) the green pastures and (where) the streams are gentle and calm...."

Naturally, there are often valid medical reasons for mood shifts and depression. And it may require all of our resources to climb back out of our private "Bad Water": support from the medical community, friends and family, as well as our spiritual resources. We are not alone.

But I also like the counsel of Abraham Lincoln, who was similarly afflicted. In a letter to a friend, he once wrote: "You cannot now believe that you will ever feel better. But this is not true. You are sure to be happy again. Knowing this, truly believing it, will make you less miserable now."

It is true that few of us seem to stay in that peaceful valley for long. But, as someone aptly said, "The truly happy person is one who can enjoy the scenery while on detour." Detours, after all, are temporary.

How Champions Are Made

Have you noticed that we usually do what we want to do?

On the day following a disaster drill, an employee made this comment in the Long Beach (California) Veteran's Administration Hospital. No kidding. The employee said, "We emptied the place in six minutes and that was pretty good, until quitting time at 4:30 when everybody got out of the building in three minutes."

English thinker and politician John Burns said, "The tragedy of (most people) is the poverty of their desires." The poverty of desire may still be the greatest kind of poverty we face worldwide. Most of us could do, have or even be practically *anything* if we simply wanted it enough.

Consider Robert Louis Stevenson. He conceived the story of Dr. Jekyll and Mr. Hyde one night when he couldn't sleep. Though bedridden with advanced tuberculosis, he wrote the whole book in three days, rarely pausing. Then, dissatisfied with the first draft, he tore it up and rewrote it in three more days! It was an unbelievable feat – he set down 64,000 words in six days; more than 10,000 words a day. Just 1,000 words a day for an accomplished writer of fiction is considered average.

I've heard it said: "Champions aren't made in the gyms. Champions are made from something they have deep inside them – a desire, a dream, a vision."

What we will accomplish is limited only by our desire. And without it, we will forever live in poverty, regardless of how much we own.

P.S.

"If you're feeling low, don't despair. Remember, the sun has a sinking spell every night, but it comes back up every morning."

Choosing the Right Compass

"We pass this way but once," we have heard it said. But my wife has learned that, unless I've studied a map, that isn't necessarily true.

So I understand the fix a local hunting guide got himself into. His party became hopelessly lost in the mountains and they blamed him for leading them astray. "You told us you were the best guide in Colorado!" they asserted.

"I am," he said, "but I think we're in Wyoming now."

It's bad enough to get lost in the city or in the mountains. But how much worse to get lost in our life's journey.

One parent asked the clerk in a discount store if they carried any compasses. She answered, "We have compasses for making circles, but not for going places." Have you ever confused the two? Has it seemed as if your life is going in circles and not actually getting anywhere? Then it may be that you are lost or at least unsure what direction you should be heading.

Here are some questions to ask yourself if you feel as if you are going in circles:

- ❖ Where do I want to be a few years from now (in this relationship, this vocation, or any other way important to me)?
- ❖ What do I need to do to make it happen?
- ❖ Who will help me along the way?
- ❖ When do I want to arrive?
- ❖ How will I take the next small step?

Living well has little to do with comfort and speed, but much to do with direction.

Powerful Dreams

Are you aware that you will miss about one-third of this coming year? You will "miss" it by sleeping. Researchers tell us that the average person sleeps about one-third of each year – or one-third of a lifetime.

But the experts also tell us that something important happens when we sleep – we dream. Apparently all people dream, even if they don't remember dreaming. And over the next twelve months, most of us will have about a thousand dreams.

Dreaming is important. But equally important are those "dreams" we have for our lives – those plans, hopes and goals we will formulate concerning our relationships, our spiritual growth, self-improvement, our physical health and our world. The dreams, or wishes, we have for our lives are just as necessary as dreaming while we sleep.

Dr. Norman Vincent Peale used to tell of a 79-year-young woman who was struck by a hit-and-run driver. She was expected to die from her injuries. When he visited, he found her wrapped in plaster from her hips to her heels. He glanced around the room, cluttered with mementos of a lifetime. He spotted a paisley shawl, a child's drawing of a horse (lavender) and shelves of much loved, much-thumbed books.

One shelf was a row of brand new books — the only new items in the room. They looked as if they had never been touched. Dr. Peale asked her if she cared for poetry. Her answer was a beautiful tribute to hope and dreams: "I love poetry, but I haven't read those yet." Her face lit up. "I'm saving them for my old age."

She did, too. She lived to read those books many times. When she finally died at 91, she was planning a trip to Europe.

Louis Driscoll put it like this: "In your heart keep one still secret spot where dreams may go, and sheltered so, may thrive and grow."

She kept her dreams alive. And they kept her alive.

P.S.

Quantum mechanics: The dreams stuff is made of.

Filled Up With Love

Welsh poet David Whyte made the intriguing observation, "I don't want to have written on my tombstone, when finally people struggle through the weeds, pull back the moss, and read the inscription there, 'He made his car payments.'"

Whyte, like most of us, wants his life to matter. Even in some small way, most people want to make a difference and, at least to some degree, they want to be happy. But it doesn't just happen.

I am inspired by the story of Rose Nelson, told in Arnold and Barry Fox's book *Making Miracles* (Emmaus, PA: The Good Spirits Press, 1989). One can usually find a cheery smile on the face of the wheelchair-bound woman. Which is remarkable, given what happened. You see, Rose was brutally beaten by two drunk teenage boys who left her unable to walk. She was forced to sell her home after medical bills devoured her modest savings.

If anyone has reason to be resentful, it is Rose Nelson. But she will smile and say that she never even thinks of being bitter as long as her brain is working and she can think of love.

"How can you be so loving after what happened to you?" she was asked.

"Oh, my," she considered. "I could have dried up after the boys beat me. I was afraid I would. That's why I decided to be full of love and to give my love to everyone. The more I love everyone else, the better I feel. And the better I feel, the more I love the world. Love cured my fear."

Rose worked at love and happiness. It had to become a high priority if she was not to be consumed by her horrific experience. Yet anyone who wants peace or happiness or joy can learn from Rose. We must do more than just make the car payments. We must love and love and love some more. Rose learned to fill her mind with as much love as it would hold, and then gave it away at every opportunity.

Dr. Karl Menninger said this about love: "We do not fall in love, we grow in love and love grows in us." Let enough grow in you to fill you up and you'll be satisfied forever.

Tell Time on Their Clock

"Find out what makes them tick, then tell time on their clock." This was one man's solution for getting along well with people. Find out what makes them tick — learn to understand them. Then tell time on their clock — identify with them and speak their language.

There is an old story which Mark Twain was said to have told first. It is about a Missouri farmer who ran five times for the state legislature without winning. It wasn't because he didn't practice his speeches. He rehearsed his campaign talks every day while milking. He referred to himself as "your humble aspirant." He referred to his audiences as "my enlightened constituents." He talked of "obtaining a mandate" for his "legislative mission."

Then one day even his cow balked at his speeches and kicked him in the teeth. With his front teeth knocked out, the farmer could speak only words of one syllable. The result was he won his next election and kept getting reelected.

However Twain felt about the electorate of his day, the story still sheds light on the importance of "telling time on their clock." A highly educated and eloquent politician may not relate to his/her constituency. Many hard working, plain folk appreciate straight talk in plain language. They distrust those who seem to "put on airs" and feel as if that candidate might just try to "put one over."

However, they can relate to one who speaks their language. This is a person who knows what makes them tick. This is someone who identifies with their plight and lets them know it.

The principle works well for non-politicians, too. If it is important to relate well to others, first learn what makes them tick. How well do you know that teenager in your life (or parent) or that client or even that supervisor? In this global community, how well do you know those of different backgrounds?

Then tell time on their clock. Let them know you understand. Speak their language. You may be amazed at the way others will respond!

P.S.

There are things more difficult to under-stand than people. Albert Einstein said, "The hardest thing in the world to understand is income tax!"

Echoes of Kind Words

A little boy said to his father, "Let's play darts. I'll throw the darts and you say, 'Wonderful!'"

Here is a boy who was not afraid to ask for the encouragement he needs. Maybe we all have something to learn from him!

Inspirational author and educator, Fr. Brian Cavanaugh, relates a story about the devastating effects of discouragement. Dante Gabriel Rossetti, the famous 19th Century poet and artist, was once approached by an elderly man who asked him to look at a few of his sketches and drawings. The gentleman wanted to know if the artist thought they were of any value.

As gently as possible, Rossetti told the man that the sketches were of no value and showed little talent. He apologized for the harsh assessment but said that he believed he should be honest.

The visitor was disappointed but asked the artist if he could take a look at just a few more, which were all done by a young art student. Rossetti looked over the second batch of sketches and immediately became enthusiastic over the talent they revealed. "These," he said, "oh, these are good." He went on to say that the young student shows much promise and should be given every help and encouragement, as he may have a great future if he will study and work hard.

The old man was deeply moved. Rossetti asked, "Who is this fine, young artist? Your son?"

"No," replied the visitor sadly. "It is I – 40 years ago. If only I had heard your praise then. For you see, I became discouraged and gave up too soon."

Mother Teresa wisely said, "Kind words can be short and easy to speak, but their echoes are truly endless." Sometimes it may be enough to just say, "Wonderful!"

The Power to Really Live

I had just graduated from college and was about to move away and pursue my dreams. An older friend said something I thought was a bit peculiar at the time. She said, "Don't ever lose your enthusiasm." I was not particularly aware that I possessed any enthusiasm, and I had no idea how to keep whatever amount I had!

But since that time, I have come to realize what she meant. Over the years, I have seen my enthusiasm assailed by discouragements and difficulties. At times I have felt totally without energy and even disenchanted with life around me.

I like what Mark Twain said about enthusiasm. When asked the reason for his success, he replied, "I was born excited." But I now know why my friend said, "Never lose your enthusiasm." For even if one is born excited, enthusiasm is easy to lose. And too many people never regain it.

However, the happiest, most fulfilled and most successful people have discovered the necessity of an enthusiastic approach to living. Thomas Edison was such a person. He was known for his energy and verve for living. He eventually acquired 1,093 patents for his inventions, including the electric light bulb, phonograph and motion picture camera. He displayed an unquenchable zeal for his work and was known to pursue it tirelessly and joyfully.

Edison eventually established Menlo Park, the first factory ever dedicated to making nothing but inventions. It was a forerunner of the private research laboratories now owned by many large corporations. Edison promised that Menlo Park would turn out a minor invention every ten days and something big every six months or so. At one point, he was working on 47 new projects at once!

Others have made more money than Thomas Edison, but none have been more enthusiastic or productive. Ralph Waldo Emerson has said, "Enthusiasm is one of the most powerful engines of success. When you do a thing, do it with your might. Put your whole soul into it. Stamp it with your own personality. Be active, be energetic, be enthusiastic and faithful, and you will accomplish your object." Enthusiasm is an engine fueled by a love for what we do. It will power us anywhere we want to go and take us places we would never reach without it!

P.S.

"You will do foolish things, but do them with enthusiasm."

The ABCs of Handling Mistakes

A grizzled old sea captain was often spotted by his crew opening a small, locked box on the bridge, peeking inside at its contents and shutting the lid before anyone might glimpse inside. The crew's curiosity grew and, on the day he retired, they rushed to the bridge, cut the lock and looked inside the box. There they found a sheet of paper that read, "Left – port. Right – starboard."

Are you afraid to make a mistake? Some people feel as if no one is ever paying attention until they make a mistake! If you goofed in a big way recently, maybe you need to hear about Roy Riegels.

The story is told about Roy and the 1929 Rose Bowl championship football game between Georgia Tech and the University of California. Shortly before halftime, a man named Roy Riegels made a huge mistake. He got the ball for California and somehow became confused and started running in the wrong direction! One of his teammates out-distanced him and tackled him after he had run 65 yards, just before he would have scored for the opposing team. Of course, Georgia Tech gained a distinct advantage through the error.

The men filed off the field and went into the dressing room. All but Riegels sat down on the benches and on the floor. He wrapped his blanket around his shoulders, sat in a corner, put his face in his hands and wept.

Coach Nibbs Price struggled with what to do with Roy. He finally looked at the team and said simply, "Men, the same team that played the first half will start the second."

All the players except Roy trotted out to the field. He didn't budge. Though the coach looked back and called to him again, he remained huddled in the corner. Coach Price went to him and said, "Roy, didn't you hear me?"

"Coach," he said, "I can't do it. I've ruined you; I've ruined the school; I've ruined myself. I couldn't face that crowd in the stadium to save my life."

But Coach Price put his hand on Riegels' shoulder and said, "Roy, get up and go on back; the game is only half over."

Roy Riegels went back and those Tech men will tell you that they have never seen a man play football as Roy Riegels played that second half.

The next time you make a mistake, it might be good to remember the ABC method of handling mistakes.

A -- Acknowledge your error and accept responsibility for it. Don't try to fix the blame on other people or circumstances. When you fix the blame, you never fix the problem.

B -- Be gentle with yourself. The game is only half over. This is not the first mistake you ever made, nor will it be the last. You are still a good and caring person. Besides, later you may laugh at the blunder, so try to lighten up a bit now.

C -- Correct it and move on. Correcting mistakes may also mean to make amends, if necessary. "Those who are wise don't consider it a blessing to make no mistakes," says Wang Yang-Ming. "They believe instead that the great virtue is the ability to correct mistakes and to continually reinvent oneself."

Now, go make your mistakes. And though some may be no less than spectacular, if you practice the ABC method, you'll live to laugh about many of them.

Autograph Your Work With Excellence

My mother used to say, "If a thing is worth doing, it is worth doing well." I am not talking about perfectionism, for "perfect" is found only in the dictionary! Those who think a thing must be perfect before it is finished will accomplish very little. I have yet to write a perfect letter, prepare a perfect meal or give a perfect speech. I admit, I've made a perfect fool of myself at times, but I wasn't trying!

Most of the time, however, my mother's admonition was on the mark. If a thing is worthy of my time, it is worthy of my best time.

In some of his speeches, Louis T. Rader relates that many top executives feel that a 99 percent effort is good enough. But here is the eye opener — if this figure (99 percent good enough) were converted into our daily non-industrial life, it means that more than 30,000 babies would be accidentally dropped by doctors and nurses each year. Electricity would be off for fifteen minutes each day.

Others have calculated that 99 percent good enough means that: 12 newborns will be given to the wrong parents daily; 114,500 mismatched pairs of shoes will be shipped each year; 18,322 pieces of mail will be mishandled per hour; 2.5 million books will be shipped with the wrong cover; two planes will crash daily at Chicago's O'Hare airport; 315 entries in Webster's Dictionary will be misspelled; and 291 pacemaker operations will be performed incorrectly.

Sometimes 99 percent really isn't good enough. Texas' first black congresswoman, Barbara Jordan, once said, "Each day you have to look into the mirror and say to yourself, 'I'm going to be the best I can no matter what it takes.'" She never said, "I will be the best." She said, "I will be the best I *can*." And it was because of her desire to be *her* best...that she became one of *our* best.

Perfect is only found in the dictionary, but doing and being one's best is an important part of a happy and fulfilled life. "Every job is a self-portrait of the person who did it," Jessica Guidobono reminds us. "Autograph your work with excellence."

P.S.

"But if you do not do good, too, then doing well will never be enough." ~ Unknown

Getting Rid of Disappointment

A great many people are disappointed because of unrealistic expectations.

Walking up to a department store's fabric counter, an attractive young woman said, "I want to buy this material for a new dress. How much does it cost?"

"Only one kiss per yard," replied the smirking male clerk.

Not to be taken back by the harassment, the woman said, "That's fine! I'll take ten yards."

With expectation and anticipation written all over his face, the clerk hurriedly measured out and wrapped the cloth, then held it out teasingly, leaning forward to receive his "payment."

The woman snapped up the package and pointed to a little old man standing beside her. "Grandpa will pay the bill," she smiled.

He was no doubt disappointed. But in the course of living, many people are disappointed when others do not live up (or down, in this case) to their expectations. In order to be happy, some expectations must be dropped. These three particular unrealistic and unhealthy expectations are some of the main culprits:

1. Do not *expect* appreciation. When others say, "Thank you," or in any way show their gratitude, be happy. It is a gift!

2. Do not *expect* others to make you happy. They simply cannot do that. Make yourself happy and share your joy with others.

3. Do not expect *not* to be let down. At times, people will simply not come through for you in the way you need. Forgive them and move on.

Get rid of these three unrealistic expectations and you can begin to expect more happiness right away!

The Guts to Fail

Someone quipped that a classified newspaper ad read: "For sale. Parachute. Only used once, never opened, small stain."

I realize that we cannot afford to fail in some endeavors. But I also know that we cannot afford *not* to fail in most of what we do. Unfortunately, too many of us live by the motto: If at first you don't succeed, don't admit that you tried. Why? We often feel ashamed or embarrassed when we fall flat.

In his book *The Courage to Fail* (McGraw-Hill, Inc. 1993), Art Mortell tells about a conversation he had with baseball's Lou Brock. It took place when Brock held the record for stolen bases. He was about 35 years old at the time and his days as a professional player were winding down. Brock was talking about why he successfully stole more bases than younger, faster players.

"When you start out in baseball," Brock said, "you're young and you have the speed and reflexes. However, when you try to steal second base and you get thrown out, it's a long walk back to the dugout, with 40,000 fans watching you. When you reach my age, you come to understand that records are not set by being the quickest, but by the willingness to look bad in the eyes of others."

There are other ways to avoid failure throughout life:

- ❖ Never ask anyone out. There will be no possibility of rejection and embarrassment.
- ❖ Never ask for a promotion. That way you will not risk the humiliation of being turned down.
- ❖ Never go back to school. You cannot fail a class you do not take.
- ❖ Never change careers. You'll never fail at something you never try.
- ❖ Never try anything you've never done before.

If success is just avoiding failure, I don't want it. But if success is about pursuing a passion or finding the guts to risk in order to experience life fully, then I want it. Even if it means a lot of long walks back to the dugout while everyone is watching.

P.S.

President Ronald Reagan once quipped, "Politics is not a bad profession. If you succeed there are many rewards; if you disgrace yourself you can always write a book."

A Little Faith

The temporary church-school teacher was struggling to open a combination lock on the supply cupboard. She thought that perhaps she'd forgotten the correct combination, so she went to the pastor's study and asked for help.

The minister came into the room and began to turn the dial. After the first two numbers he paused and stared blankly for a moment. Then he lifted his eyes upward and whispered something too faint to be heard. He finally turned back to the lock, entered the final number and opened it.

The teacher was amazed. "I'm in awe at your faith, Pastor," she said.

"It's really nothing," he answered. "The number is taped to the ceiling."

Of course, he still may have been a man of great faith. Or he may have been a man of little faith. Not that it matters, for even a little faith can move a mountain-sized obstacle.

Often, if we just begin with a tiny bit of belief and fertilize it with desire, even some of the most impossible obstacles imaginable can be surmounted and some of the most outlandish aspirations can be realized. Just a little belief, firmly held, can accomplish a great thing.

Many Warsaw Jews died during the German occupation of their city during World War II. But some survived, and some were sustained by faith. During those dark years, an unknown hand wrote this graffiti on a Warsaw ghetto wall:

I believe in the sun, even if it does not shine.
I believe in love, even if I do not feel it.
I believe in God, even if I do not see Him.

Faith, little or great, can make a big difference.

Six Traits of Healthy Families

It takes some adjusting to live in a family. Like changing your attitudes about children and the kitchen. I used to by picky. But my philosophy now is – if it walks out of the refrigerator, let it go!

Some people never make the adjustments. George Burns used to say, "Happiness is having a large, loving, caring, close-knit family in another city." But for most of us, happiness is making the most of our family life, in whatever form and shape that family exists.

Family consultant Dolores Curran published what she considered "Traits of a Healthy Family" (Mass Market Paperback, 1984), drawn from responses of more than 500 professionals who work with families. Here are a few of the top qualities shared by families considered "healthy."

❖ **Communication and listening. Are you working at this?**

❖ Affirmation and support. A southern (USA) migrant worker told a sociologist that "home is a place to go back to if things get rough out there." If you cannot receive affirmation at home, where else are you going to get it?

❖ A sense of play. Charlie Shedd says, "Whenever parents ask me, 'How can I keep my children off drugs?' I say, 'Have fun.'"

❖ Shared responsibility. Everyone helps out; everyone pitches in.

❖ Trust. The fastest way to drive a wedge between family members is to violate it.

❖ Shared religious core. Does your family share similar spiritual goals?

Follow these six traits to make the most of your family life!

P.S.

One woman said her family is like fudge... mostly sweet with a few nuts....

A Monster to Hug

One couple spent a holiday driving in the mountains. "Every time you race around one of those narrow curves," exclaimed the wife, "I just get terrified."

"Then do what I do," suggested her husband. "Close your eyes!"

We are all afraid at times, but closing our eyes is not always a helpful way through fear. Better to open your eyes and face those fears head-on.

In 1972 David Miln Smith had such an opportunity. Smith, an adventurer, author and professional speaker, decided to spend a night alone in St. Michael's Cave on the island of Gibraltar as a test of courage. In his book *Hug the Monster* (Kansas City: Andrews and McMeel, 1996), he tells of hearing strange sounds all around him as he lay there in the pitch-black, damp, deserted cave. Most frightening was the fact that he came to believe he was not alone!

Fear became panic and he was afraid he was losing his mind. Then suddenly, as he was approaching his psychological breaking point, Smith thought to himself, "Whatever the monster looks like, I will hug it." That simple, almost silly thought brought great relief to his restless mind. He soon fell into a deep and peaceful sleep until morning. He learned that embracing his fear, literally or figuratively, allowed him to subdue it.

We each have our nights of fear. We each encounter monsters of some sort. We may fear spiders or insects, heights or crowds, abandonment or loneliness, the future or death. And most of us are occasionally visited by shadows of these monsters in the dark of night.

The next time you're afraid, try "hugging the monster." Face that fear head-on, whatever it is, and embrace it. You may be surprised at how quickly it slips away and at how confident you begin to feel. Like that beautiful spirit Eleanor Roosevelt said, "You gain strength, courage, and confidence by every experience in which you stop to look fear in the face."

Do you have a monster to hug?

You are Gifted

A story concerns itself with a wholesaler in New York who sent a letter to the postmaster of a small Midwestern town. He asked for the name of an honest lawyer who would take a collection case against a local debtor who had refused to pay for a shipment of the wholesaler's goods. He got this reply:

> *Dear Sir:*
> *I am the postmaster of this village and received your letter. I am also an honest lawyer and ordinarily would be pleased to accept a case against a local debtor. In this case, however, I also happen to be the person you sold those crummy goods to. I received your demand to pay and refused to* ·
> *honor it. I am also the banker you sent the draft to draw on the merchant, and I sent that back with a note stating that the mer-*

chant had refused to pay. And if I were not, for the time being, substituting for the pastor of our local church, I would tell you just where to stick your claim.

Not many of us are multi-talented. We cannot do *all* things well, or even fairly well. You may be a skilled chef, for example. Or, on the other hand, your motto may be more like mine: "Where there's smoke, there's dinner."

As gifted as the great mathematician was, even Albert Einstein experienced feelings of inadequacy. In 1948 Einstein was offered the first presidency of the new nation of Israel. He turned it down with this statement: "I know little about the nature of people.... And I am saddened and ashamed that I cannot accept it.... I lack both the natural aptitude and the experience to deal properly with people."

Dr. Einstein knew plenty about the nature of the universe, but this wise and sensitive man also knew that he lacked the necessary political skill for such a demanding position. Is there really any shame in knowing our limitations? He focused on that which he did well and the world is the better for it.

You may not recognize it, but you are gifted for something! Whether it be big or small, do what you are gifted to do and you will be happy.

P.S.

Speaking of skills and abilities, comedian Conan O'Brien quipped: "A study in the Washington Post says that women have better verbal skills than men. I just want to say to the authors of that study, 'Duh.'"

Hooked on Giving

Dr. Mar Aprem of the ancient Chaldean Orthodox Church of the East in India tells a funny story about when a member of the church won a lottery worth 100,000 rupees. His wife went to the bishop and told him that she was afraid to tell this glad news to her husband because he had a heart problem and any sudden excitement could cause a heart attack.

The bishop offered to break the news gently to her husband. He visited the house and asked the man, "Wouldn't it be a good thing if you won 1,000 rupees in the lottery?" The man replied that he still would have to work to support his family.

"What about 10,000 rupees?" the bishop asked. The man still showed no excitement, so the bishop carefully raised the amount to 50,000 and finally to 100,000 rupees.

"If I got 100,000 rupees, I would give half of it to you, your Excellency," the man replied.

The bishop had a heart attack, and the man called an ambulance.

We can get excited about winning and getting. But have you learned how fun it is to give? Engineering and machinery genius R. G. LeTourneau discovered the joy of generosity. Besides establishing a private school, he reportedly gave 90 percent of his income to worthwhile causes, while living on the remaining 10 percent. He became hooked on the fun of giving!

Of course, money is not the only commodity that is fun to give. Give some time, give your expertise, give a smile or give your love. You can never run out of something worthwhile to give.

Giving is fun. And there is no stopping those who discover it!

Eyes on the Shore

A story is told about a bloodhound chasing a stag. A fox crossed the path, so the hound chased the fox. After a while a rabbit crossed the path, so the hound chased it. Later, a mouse crossed the path and the hound chased the mouse into a hole. The hound began his hunt on the trail of a magnificent stag and ended up watching a mouse hole!

Not that there is anything wrong with spontaneity. Some of the most wonderful things may come into our lives by beautiful accident. But there is also something to be said for knowing where we want to go.

Florence Chadwick learned the importance of keeping a goal in mind on July 4, 1952. She waded into the Pacific Ocean off Catalina Island and began swimming toward the California coast 26 miles away. The day was cold and her attendants drove off sharks throughout the journey.

Florence had already swum the English Channel twice and, if she could finish today, she would be the first woman to have swum both. But after fifteen hours in the water, for the first and only time in her long-distance swimming career, she gave up and climbed into the escort boat. Others had urged her on, but in the fog they could not tell her how near she was to the coast. She later learned that she was less than half a mile from shore.

When asked by a reporter why she gave up, Florence replied: "It was the fog. If I could have seen land, I could have finished. But when you can't see your goal, you lose all sense of progress and you begin to give up."

On a warm, sunny day two months later Florence Chadwick swam the Catalina Channel, handily beating the men's record. Only when she kept her eyes on her goal did she eventually arrive there.

Keeping that goal constantly in sight will get you where you want to go.

P.S.

"Don't give up when you still have something to give."

Higher Power

A Sunday school teacher said to her children: "We have been learning how powerful kings and queens were in Bible times. But there is a higher power. Can anybody tell me what it is?"

One child blurted out, "Aces!"

Card games aside, a higher power is recognized around the world by those of faith.

I attended theology school and caught a glimpse of that higher power in an unusual way. One year I enrolled in a large seminar of about seventy-five students. On the first day of class Dr. Justo Gonzalez called roll and momentarily studied each person who raised a hand in attendance. After roll call he quipped that he will not be calling roll any more, but will remember our names as long as we "wear the same shirt to class."

Two days later I approached Dr. Gonzalez with a question. Before I could utter a word, he said, "Yes, Mr. Goodier, may I help you?" He recognized me – and I had changed shirts!

Dr. Gonzalez taught more than 150 students each ten-week quarter, yet he remembered my name and never forgot it.

I have often thought it admirable that one in his position *cared* enough about all his students to memorize their names. To him, not one student was unnoticed or unimportant. Regardless of whatever else he tried to teach about theology and a higher power, I will always remember that he called me by name. For more than anything else, that gave me a glimpse into the heart of God.

Be Glad Today

Yesterday I brought home an Easter lily I found while shopping. I once read that those beautiful and fragrant flowers were named because of their shape! The blossom looks like a trumpet, and trumpets have long been used to announce good news.

There is plenty of *bad* news all around. I came across an article that reported a study of a large group of people who were instructed to evaluate all the information they received for a year and a half. They were asked to record whether what they were seeing and hearing all day long was positive or negative. These researchers determined that ninety percent of the input the group received was negative!

That may not come as a surprise to everyone. Over a half-century ago, Franklin Roosevelt told about an old man who was losing his hearing and went to the doctor for help. He was advised to quit drinking alcohol. When his family asked him what he was going to do, he replied, "Well, I've given it a lot of thought and I've decided I like what I've been drinkin' so much better than what I've been hearin', I'm just gonna keep on gettin' deaf."

There is plenty of bad news. But there is also *good* news. Lots of it. And the closer we look around, the more good news we find. In fact, every day should be a day to share life, love and laughter.

So let the trumpets sound and the bells ring. Celebrate and be glad! And...share some good news.

P.S.

A sign in the front yard of a funeral home reads: "Drive carefully, we'll wait."

Driving Nails

Desiderius Erasmus has said, "A nail is driven out by another nail. Habit is overcome by habit." We should not simply resist "bad habits," we would do better to create good ones.

A teacher who was lecturing on habits told his class, "Anything you repeat twenty times is yours forever." From the back of the classroom came a whispered voice, "Amanda...Amanda... Amanda...Amanda...."

What the teacher was trying to say is that any behavior, often repeated, becomes habit. And any habit, often repeated, becomes stronger and more powerful. Which is why Dr. E. Stanley Jones was so wise in admonishing us, "Since habits become power, make them work for you and not against you." In other words, drive out the undesirable nail with a good one.

One woman did just that after lamenting to her friend, "I hate being late. It has been a problem for me all of my life."

"Do you really want to change that habit?" her friend asked. The woman said that she did and her friend responded, "All right. Every time you are late for work or anywhere else, you must give me $25."

"I would go broke!" came the reply. "But I will do $10."

"It has to be a large enough amount of money for it to hurt," said the friend.

"Believe me, that will hurt," the woman replied. They agreed that the money should be deposited in a jar and used for charity.

In the first week, the habitually tardy woman only paid $10 to her friend. The next week, $20. The third week, none at all. By week five, she had built a new habit that changed an irritating pattern that had hindered her all of her life. She drove out one nail with another one, and in doing so she found freedom.

Behaviors, as well as attitudes, often repeated, become strong habits. And great freedom is found in replacing that unwanted way of acting or thinking with one you choose. It is an important piece of a whole and happy life.

P.S.

Francis Picabia said, "Our heads are round so our thinking can change direction."

No One to Call

One afternoon after the death of her grandfather, Carol lay huddled on her bed, sobbing forlornly. Her mother sat beside her and asked, "What's the matter, honey?"

"I miss my grandpa, and I miss talking to him about my problems," the girl said.

"I know, dear," sympathized her mother. "I miss him too. But can't you talk to me?" Carol shook her head vehemently.

"Why not?" her mother persisted.

"Because you're what we talked about," sobbed Carol.

Children may not confide in their parents, however much Mom and Dad may like them to. And adults may choose not to discuss problems with many of their friends, co-workers and distant family. But it is important to have *someone* with whom we can be emotionally intimate.

Yet it has been estimated that the majority of men, and many women, have nobody they could call at 2:00 in the morning if their lives fall apart. Nobody that would want to hear from them in a crisis. It seems that, outside our immediate families, too many of us are utterly without intimacy.

The philosopher Goethe once observed, "The world is so empty if one thinks only of mountains, rivers and cities; but to know someone here and there who thinks and feels with us, and who, though distant, is close to us in spirit, this makes the earth an inhabited garden."

Who can you be vulnerable with? Is the earth, for you, more like a lonely desert or an inhabited garden? The difference may simply be in whom you feel free to call at your most wounded moments. Do you have such a person? And are you such a person for someone else?

As it has been said, "A friend is someone who knows the song in your heart and can sing it back to you when you have forgotten the words." If we are to find the kind of friend who knows the song in our hearts, we must also *be* that kind of friend. And since good friends take time to grow — we'd better get started!

P.S.

Oscar Wilde quipped, "A good friend stabs you in the front."

Health Insurance

Have you noticed how health insurance is like a hospital gown: every time you turn around, you find something that isn't covered? But health researchers are now discovering what many people have known all along – that getting healthy is about more than medicine and treatment. It also involves a healthy outlook on life.

Various studies have validated the mind/body connection. Cancer is often diagnosed within months of the death of one's spouse. People who are cynical or angry have been shown to be more prone to heart attacks than those with a more positive outlook. And former *Saturday Evening Post* editor Norman Cousins has demonstrated for years how humor, laughter and hope can aid the healing process.

Not only is a healthy mental outlook necessary, but a healthy spiritual outlook seems to be equally important. Noted psychologist Carl Jung

(1865-1961) made a telling observation about the connection between one's mental health and spiritual outlook. "During the past 30 years, people from all civilized countries of the earth have consulted me," he said. "Among all my patients in the second half of life – that is to say, over 35 – there has not been one whose problem in the last resort was not that of finding a (spiritual) outlook on life. It is safe to say that every one of them fell ill because he (or she) had lost that which living religions of every age have given to their followers...."

It seems that a healthy mental and spiritual outlook, like eating, sleeping and paying taxes, is not really an option. Not when one is looking for wholeness!

Who's Your Hero?

One of those strange newspaper stories told of a 19-year-old woman who had been charged in Los Angeles with two counts of trespassing, after sneaking into the home of actor Brad Pitt and trying on his clothes. I suppose we have different ways of adoring our heroes....

But who are our real heroes? I was given a little quiz recently. See how well you do:

Name the five wealthiest people in the world. Name five Olympic gold medalists. Name the last five winners of your national beauty contest. Name ten people who have won the Nobel or Pulitzer Prize. Name the last half-dozen Academy Award winners for best actor and actress. Name the last decade's national or world champions in your favorite sport.

These people, of course, are the best in their fields. But fame is fleeting and outstanding performance is too soon forgotten.

Now try another quiz: List a few teachers who aided your journey through school. Name three friends who have helped you through a difficult time. Name five people who have taught you something worthwhile. Think of a few people who have made you feel appreciated and special. Think of five people you enjoy spending time with. Name half a dozen heroes whose stories have inspired you.

If you found the second quiz easier, it may be because those people who make a difference in our lives are not the ones with the best degrees or pedigrees, nor are they the most honored or honorable. The people who make a difference are those who care. They may never have seen a battle; never scored a winning goal; never been featured in a magazine. But they have been busy helping you to be the best you can be.

Let's remember and thank our real heroes. And don't be surprised if someone thanks you.

P.S.

Another take on heroism: "A boy doesn't have to go to war to be a hero; he can say he doesn't like pie when he sees there isn't enough to go around." ~ Edgar Watson Howe

You Have a Chance

Charles Revson, founder of the successful cosmetic manufacturing firm Revlon, once said, "In our factory we make lipstick. In our advertising, we sell hope."

Smart advertisers know that one thing people the world round need is hope. Hence the popularity of lottery tickets. One poor mother, who was raising her children on a small salary earned from long hours of hard work, was asked, "Why do you waste your money on a lottery ticket when you can hardly make ends meet?"

"Yeah, I buy a ticket every day," the woman acknowledged. "But a dollar is not too much to pay for 24 hours of hope." Though gambling on the lottery will usually disappoint, like all of us, this woman needs hope.

Hope is a vital ingredient to life. Without it, far too many people come to the conclusion that their life is simply not worth living and finally give up. When hope is gone, they have nothing left.

Norman Cousins, in *Head First, the Biology of Hope* (Penguin USA, 1990), illustrates the power of hope. He tells of two physicians who were to deliver a paper at a national meeting of cancer specialists. One was complaining bitterly, "I don't understand it, Bob. We use the same drugs, the same dosage, and the same schedule of treatment. Yet I get a 22% recovery rate and you get a 74% recovery rate. How do you explain that?"

The other responded, "We both use Etoposide, Platinol, Oncovin, and Hydroxyurea. You put those letters together and tell people that you are giving them EPOH. I put them together and explain to them that they are receiving HOPE. I emphasize that they have a chance."

You have a chance! You have a chance at *life*. You have a chance at success. You have a chance at wholeness. You have a chance at meaningful relationships and, though you may not believe it, at happiness!

Don't give up, for with the help of God and sufficient hope, you have that chance you need.

A Humble Spirit

In his own eyes, Mike was the most popular guy around. "A lot of women are gonna be totally miserable when I marry," he boasted to his date.

"Really?" she said. "And just how many women are you intending to marry?"

What passes for conceit in many people is often just a plea for attention. A poor sense of self may cause one to want to be the prominent star in every constellation. Humility, on the other hand, does not require that one shine *less* brightly than others, simply that all be given opportunity to shine.

That great African American educator Booker T. Washington exemplified the beauty of a humble spirit. James Moore tells us in his book *Standing on the Promise or Sitting on the Premises* (Dimensions for Living, 1995) that one day as Professor Washington was walking to work at Tuskegee Institute in Alabama, he happened to pass the mansion of a wealthy woman.

The woman, who did not recognize him, called out, "Hey you! Come here! I need some wood chopped!" She was a product of her culture and simply perceived him as a black man who was there to do her bidding.

Without a word, Dr. Washington peeled off his jacket, picked up the ax and went to work. He not only cut a large pile of wood, he also carried the firewood into the house and arranged it neatly.

He had scarcely left when a servant said to the woman, "I guess you didn't recognize him, ma'am, but that was Professor Washington!"

Embarrassed and ashamed, the woman hurried over to Tuskegee Institute to apologize. The great educator humbly replied: "There's no need to apologize, madam. I'm delighted to do favors for my friends!"

The professor taught a marvelous lesson that day. He felt no need to convince her that he, too, was a bright star in the constellation.

Author Ken Blanchard puts it this way: "Humility does not mean you think less of yourself. It means you think of yourself less."

P.S.

"There are two ways to live your life. One is as though nothing is a miracle. The other is as though everything is a miracle." ~ *Albert Einstein*

Admitting Our Schnozzles

A humorous story has it that many generations ago, a soldier was sentenced to be flogged. As if something hilarious were about to happen, he chuckled as they led him away and laughed uproariously throughout the whipping.

When the painful punishment finally ended, the officer in charge demanded, "What's so funny about a flogging? I don't think it's a joke."

"Why, the joke's on you," smiled the soldier. "I'm the wrong man!"

Of course, no one would really laugh through a flogging, even if one were to see a humorous side to the situation. But isn't it true that there just might be a funny side to almost anything you and I are experiencing? Do you look for that funny side?

Comedian Jimmy Durante was known for his prominent nose. He once said, "It dawned on me that as long as I could laugh, I was safe from the world; and I have learned since that laughter keeps

149

me safe from myself, too. All of us have schnozzles that are ridiculous in one way or another; if not in our faces, then in our characters, minds or habits. When we admit our schnozzles, instead of defending them, we begin to laugh and the world laughs with us."

Sounds like a secret to happiness!

Who Do You Think You Are?

The Houston Post carried an article about a man the Dutch police arrested in the town of Rosendaal. They found him in possession of 186 false papers, including 29 Nigerian passports, 30 British passports, 74 Dutch work permits, 12 British driving licenses, 18 birth or death certificates, 2 British student cards, an international driving license and 20 forged checks. They said that the man had not yet been conclusively identified!

A humorist said, "I go to this doctor and pay him 75 dollars an hour, and all he does is ask me the same question my father used to ask me all the time: 'Who do you think you are, anyway?'" Not a bad question, actually.

I think I spent the first 20 or 30 years of my life wondering who I really was. I thought I'd never know what to study in school and I was sure I'd never figure out what kind of person I might be happy spending my life with. Then, just when I thought I knew myself fairly well, I changed! And through the years I changed again. And again! It seems like I've always been up against the question, "Who do you think you are?"

I appreciate Benjamin Kubelski's story. In 1902, his father gave him a violin for his eighth birthday. It cost $50, a small fortune in those days, and especially for a recently immigrated Russian family.

Benjamin did well and was playing concerts as a teenager. At age 18 he teamed up with a woman pianist as a musical team in Vaudeville.

But he suspected the violin did not satisfy his heart's desire. Then one night, Benjamin impulsively decided to tell the audience about a funny incident that had happened during the day. He later said, "The audience laughed and the sound intoxicated me. That laughter ended my days as a musician." And it began his life career as the comedian Jack Benny.

He found who he was and everything fit into place. He knew that if he followed his heart's desire, he would end up all right.

You and I may never know ourselves conclusively. But listen to your heart. Listen for that still, small voice within and make up your mind to follow. I don't know where you will end up, but it will be all right.

P.S.

Wil Courter says correctly, "A sense of humor is a sense of proportion."

A Spittin' Image

A young mother enlisted the help of a friend in taking her infant identical twins to the doctor. Since the waiting area was full, the two women, each with a twin, were seated on opposite sides of the room. After a few minutes someone commented, "It's amazing how much those two babies look alike!"

The friend was quick to reply, "Well, they should. They have the same father." I haven't heard whether the misunderstanding was ever straightened out....

One might say these babies were the "spittin' image" of each other. That term, "spittin' image," stems from an old misunderstanding itself. Joel Chandler Harris, author of the Uncle Remus stories, explained that when an American slave seemed to be saying, "spittin' image," he or she was actually saying, "spirit and image," as: "'He's the spi'it 'n' image of his daddy."

Spirit and image. Fascinating, isn't it? And what makes it even more interesting is the truth from St. Bernard of Clairvaux, who said, "What we love we shall grow to resemble." Or put another way, we become the spirit and image of that which we hold dear, at least on the inside.

Since we become like that which we most love, we want to choose whom and what to love very carefully. Where to place those priorities. How to devote our best time and energy. To whom we give our fullest attention. For love is about these things of the heart, and our spirits will resemble that which has hold of the heart.

Just Imagine That!

Three-year-old Jonathon is gifted. And pre-cocious.

When his parents took him to a restaurant, he ordered a grilled cheese sandwich.

"Jonathon, I'm sorry, we don't serve grilled cheese sandwiches," the server replied.

He asked playfully, "You have a grill, don't you?"

She answered, "Yes."

He continued, "You have cheese, don't you?"

"Yes, we do."

"You have bread, don't you?"

"Yes.

"Well," he said, "I'll have a grilled cheese sandwich."

Three years old. (You may think his parents should have taught him better manners, but please don't miss the marvel of this small child's imagination.)

The smiling server returned after checking with the chef and told the boy they would be happy to fix him the sandwich. "But I forgot to ask you what you want to drink," she said.

"I'll have a milkshake, please."

"I'm sorry, Jonathon, but we don't serve milkshakes," she answered. But this time she was ready for him. "Now, it is true we have milk. And it is true we have ice cream. But we don't have syrup," she explained.

He laughed, "You have a car, don't you?"

Whatever other intellectual gifts Jonathon exhibits, the trait that may serve him best is imagination. We're told that Albert Einstein said, "Imagination is everything. It is the preview of life's coming attractions." He also said, "Imagination is more important than knowledge." And Napoleon is purported to have said, "Imagination rules the world."

I have come to realize that I am limited only by my imagination. When I believe nothing can be done, I search for a way out when I could do better searching for solutions. When I perceive my situation as impossible, I resign myself to that fate when I might be drawing upon greater resources of faith and courage. I far too often settle for less when I

157

could be asking myself that transformative question, "What if...?"

The truth is, if it can be imagined, it can come to be. The solution to your problem, the way through your dilemma or the answer to your yearning must first be conceived in your mind before it can be birthed in life. Conceive it and believe it, then you will achieve it.

Just imagine that!

P.S.

"The nice thing about egotists is that they don't talk about other people." ~ Lucille S. Harper

Beyond the Humps

A police officer told an all-too-common story. While on patrol, she was pleased one day to see a car sporting a bumper sticker that read, "Hang up and drive." She had witnessed too many accidents caused by motorists talking on cell phones.

Wanting to signal her approval to the driver, she pulled up alongside the car. When she glanced over, however, she was dismayed to see a man peering into his rear-view mirror -- while shaving! His crusade against using the phone while driving had apparently not extended to driving and shaving.

An African proverb states, "The camel never sees its own hump, but that of its brother is always before its eyes." And with humans, when those irritating faults of others are constantly before our eyes, we can likewise let them obscure our vision. We soon lose sight of the good and decent qualities of another, the true essence of who they are, and all we see is the "hump."

So what will you look at? Will you notice only so-called humps, or will you look beyond them to love and goodness? A good question to ask yourself is, "Do I choose to be a love finder or a fault finder?" For we can't do one while we're busy doing the other.

Prescription for Peace

Many years ago, Dr. A. J. Cronin occasionally prescribed an unusual treatment for some of his patients who were feeling "blue," "down," or generally blah. He would insist that for six weeks the patient say, "Thank you" for every kindness and keep a record of it. According to Dr. Cronin, he had a remarkable cure rate!

If you find yourself depressed, please consult your medical doctor. But everyone gets down at times, and sharpening your sense of gratitude can make an important difference in the way you feel.

Writer Arthur Gordon (*Daily Guideposts*, October 1983) told about asking a physician friend of his for the name of the most effective prescription he knew.

"Well, I'll tell you," his friend said. "A colleague of mine once had a woman patient who suffered from depression. Got to the point where she stayed at home all the time, listless, apathetic, indifferent to just about everything. The usual medications didn't seem to help.

One day this doctor delivered a small package to the woman's home. "I want you to take what's in this package," he said, "and spend ten minutes of every day looking through it at some object in this room."

In the package there was a strong magnifying glass. The woman began looking through it at the warp and woof of the fabric on her sofa. She was amazed at what she saw! Then she examined the veins in a flower plucked from her garden, the color dots in an old photograph, and even the texture of her own skin. That was the turning point of her illness. She began to get well because the doctor and his "prescription" had aroused the most curative of all emotions – gratitude.

Sharpening your sense of gratitude is no less than a powerful prescription for peace.

Index

Index, cont.